# Walt Whitman's Diary:
# A Summer in Canada

Edited by Harriet Hungerford

*"It is only here in large portions of Canada that wondrous second wind, the Indian summer, attains its amplitude and heavenly perfection, the temperature; the sunny haze; the mellow, rich, delicate, almost flavored air:*

*"Enough to live, enough to merely be."*

# CONTENTS

Introduction: When The Diary Starts    Page v

The Diary    Page 1
What Next? Whitman's Life After The Diary Ends    Page 43
The Life Of The Diary Itself    Page 48
This Edition    Page 51
Map, Photographs And Footnotes    Page 52

# INTRODUCTION:
# WHEN THE DIARY STARTS

Walt Whitman's diary of a summer in Canada begins on Friday June 4th, 1880. This is the first full day of his trip and comes a few days after his 61st birthday.

Having first published his famous, long poem 'Leaves of Grass' 25 years before, Whitman is by this time well-established as the much-loved and much-hated American poet of the age. He is revered by leading literary figures such as Emerson, Thoreau, Tennyson and Oscar Wilde who found joy in his "free and brave thought". He is reviled by others for his obscenity, sacked, excluded and the distribution of his poems banned in some states.

In 1880 Whitman describes himself to friends as "a half-paralytic". He had suffered a severe stroke 7 years before and been much troubled by his health ever since. This trip into Canada — his first and only long trip to a foreign country — must have felt a great risk as well as a great adventure. A couple of days before he leaves, Whitman makes a new will, dividing his $1800[i] estate between family members. He is living in his brother George's small house in Camden, New Jersey just across the bridge from Philadelphia, along with George[ii] himself, George's wife Louisa[iii] and another brother Eddie[iv], who has learning disabilities.

Whitman's summer in Canada is to be spent in the company of his friend Dr. Richard Maurice Bucke[v]. Some years before, having felt a deep connection to Whitman's work, Dr. Bucke wrote to Whitman to say so and a deep friendship had developed from there. At the time of the diary, Maurice Bucke is running the Asylum for the Insane in London, Ontario and is a pioneer of progressive, sympathetic treatments for the mentally ill. Whitman and Bucke had discussed the possibility of Bucke's writing a biography of Whitman and this planned summer time together is partly to give them an opportunity to work on that, as well as to explore eastern Canada.

As a result of his health troubles, Whitman looks older than his years, an impressive, prophet-like figure with long gray hair and beard.

Bucke describes his appearance in 1880:

*"At first sight he looked much older so that he was often supposed to be seventy or eighty. He is six feet in height, and quite straight. He weighs nearly two hundred pounds...*

*The eyebrows are highly arched, so that it is a long distance from the eye to the centre of the eyebrow — (this is the facial feature that strikes one most at first sight). The eyes themselves are light blue, not large, — indeed in proportion to the head and face they seemed to me rather small; they are dull and heavy, not expressive — what expression they have is kindness, composure, suavity...*

*His complexion is peculiar, a bright maroon tint, which, contrasting with his white hair and beard, makes an impression very striking...*

*Walt Whitman's dress was always extremely plain. He usually wore in pleasant weather a light gray suit of good woollen cloth. The only thing peculiar about his dress that he had no neck-tie at any time, and always wore shirts with very large turn-down collars, the button at the neck some five or six inches lower than usual, so that the throat and upper part of the breast were exposed. In all other respects he dressed in a substantial, neat, plain, common way. Everything he wore, and everything about him, was always scrupulously clean. His clothes might (and often did) show signs of wear, or they might be torn or have holes in them; but they never looked soiled..."*

*Whitman in 1880*

Bucke himself is 43 at the time and not in peak physical condition, having lost a foot and several toes to frostbite in a silver mining expedition in his early 20s.

*Bucke, date unknown*

Whitman and Bucke — this pair of slightly unlikely adventurers — start their time together a few days before the diary begins. On May 25th, 1880 Bucke arrives in Camden and remains there a few days before the two set off together for Bucke's home in London, Ontario in the evening of Thursday, June 3rd.

The full journey of their summer travels is shown here.

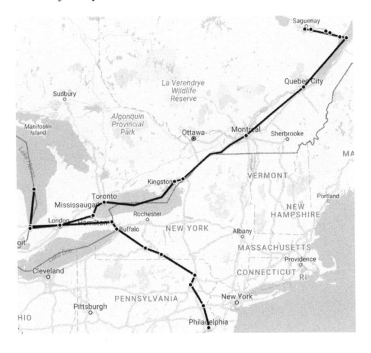

# THE DIARY

## Friday, June 4th, 1880
## Buffalo, New York, and London, Ontario

Buffalo, noon, Friday.

All right, so far — had a good trip & a good sleeper & bed & accommodations — best RR track I ever travelled over — had good breakfast at 8 at Hornellsville — am now about 430 miles from Phila: I believe — am feeling all right

*Later the same day.*

Jaunting to Canada

To go back a little, I left Philadelphia, 9th and Green streets[vi], at 8 o'clock P.M., June 3, on a first-class sleeper, by the Lehigh Valley (North Pennsylvania) route, through Bethlehem, Wilkesbarre, Waverly, and so (by Erie) on through Corning to Hornellsville, where we arrived at 8, morning, and had a bounteous breakfast. I must say I never put in such a good night on any railroad track — smooth, firm, the minimum of jolting, and all the swiftness compatible with safety. So without change to Buffalo, and thence to Clifton, where we arrived early afternoon; then on to London, Ontario, Canada, in four more — less than twenty-two hours altogether. I am domiciled at the hospitable house of my friends Dr. and Mrs. Bucke, in the ample and charming garden and lawns of the asylum.[vii]

*Dr Bucke's house at the London Asylum for the Insane, Ontario*

## Seeing Niagara to advantage

For really seizing a great picture or book, or piece of music, or architecture, or grand scenery — or perhaps for the first time even the common sunshine, or landscape, or may-be even the mystery of identity, most curious mystery of all — there comes some lucky five minutes of a man's life, set amid a fortuitous concurrence of circumstances, and bringing in a brief flash the culmination of years of reading and travel and thought. The present case about two o'clock this afternoon, gave me Niagara, its superb severity of action and color and majestic grouping, in one short, indescribable show. We were very slowly crossing the Suspension bridge — not a full stop anywhere, but next to it — the day clear, sunny, still — and I out on the platform. The falls were in plain view about a mile off, but very distinct, and no roar — hardly a murmur. The river tumbling green and white, far below me; the dark high banks, the plentiful umbrage, many bronze cedars, in shadow; and tempering and arching all the immense materiality, a clear sky overhead, with a few white clouds, limpid, spiritual, silent. Brief, and as quiet as brief, that picture — a remembrance always afterwards. Such are the things, indeed, I lay away with my life's rare and blessed bits of hours, reminiscent, past — the wild sea-storm I once saw one winter day, off Fire island — the elder Booth in Richard, that famous night forty years ago in the old Bowery[viii]— or Alboni in the children's scene in Norma[ix]— or night-views, I remember, on the field, after battles in Virginia — or the peculiar sentiment of moonlight and stars over the great Plains, western Kansas — or scooting up New York bay, with a stiff breeze and a good yacht, off Navesink. With these, I say, I henceforth place that view, that afternoon, that combination complete, that five minutes' perfect absorption of Niagara — not the great majestic gem alone by itself, but set complete in all its varied, full, indispensable surroundings.

**Sunday, June 6th, 1880**
**London, Ontario**

<u>Sunday with the insane</u>

Went over to the religious services (Episcopal) main Insane asylum, held in a lofty, good-sized hall, third story. Plain boards, whitewash, plenty of cheap chairs, no ornament or color, yet all scrupulously clean and sweet. Some three hundred persons present, mostly patients. Everything, the prayers, a short sermon, the firm, orotund voice of the minister, and most of all, beyond any portraying, or suggesting, that audience, deeply impress'd me. I was furnish'd with an arm-chair near the pulpit, and sat facing the motley, yet perfectly well-behaved and orderly congregation. The quaint dresses and bonnets of some of the women, several very old and gray, here and there like the heads in old pictures. O the looks that came from those faces! There were two or three I shall probably never forget. Nothing at all markedly repulsive or hideous — strange enough

I did not see one such. Our common humanity, mine and yours, everywhere:

"The same old blood — the same red, running blood;"

yet behind most, an inferr'd arriere of such storms, such wrecks, such mysteries, fires, love, wrong, greed for wealth, religious problems, crosses — mirror'd from those crazed faces (yet now temporarily so calm, like still waters,) all the woes and sad happenings of life and death — now from every one the devotional element radiating — was it not, indeed, the peace of God that passeth all understanding, strange as it may sound? I can only say that I took long and searching eyesweeps as I sat there, and it seem'd so, rousing unprecedented thoughts, problems unanswerable. A very fair choir, and melodeon accompaniment. They sang 'Lead, kindly light,' after the sermon. Many join'd in the beautiful hymn, to which the minister read the introductory text, In the daytime also He led them with a cloud, and all the night with a light of fire. Then the words:

Lead, kindly light, amid the encircling gloom,
Lead thou me on.
The night is dark, and I am far from home;
Lead thou me on.
Keep thou my feet; I do not ask to see
The distant scene; one step enough for me.

I was not ever thus, nor pray'd that thou
Should'st lead me on;
I lov'd to choose and see my path; but now
Lead thou me on.
I loved the garish day, and spite of fears
Pride ruled my will; remember not past years.

A couple of days after, I went to the Refractory building, under special charge of Dr. Beemer[x], and through the wards pretty thoroughly, both the men's and women's. I have since made many other visits of the kind through the asylum, and around

4

among the detach'd cottages. As far as I could see, this is among the most advanced, perfected, and kindly and rationally carried on, of all its kind in America. It is a town in itself, with many buildings and a thousand inhabitants.

I learn that Canada, and especially this ample and populous province, Ontario, has the very best and plentiest benevolent institutions in all departments.

**Tuesday, June 8ᵗʰ, 1880**
**London, Ontario**

Reminiscence of Elias Hicks[xi]

To-day a letter from Mrs. E. S. L.[xii], Detroit, accompanied in a little post-office roll by a rare old engraved head of Elias Hicks, (from a portrait in oil by Henry Inman, painted for J. V. S., must have been 60 years or more ago, in New York) — among the rest the following excerpt about E. H. in the letter:

"I have listen'd to his preaching so often when a child, and sat with my mother at social gatherings where he was the centre, and every one so pleas'd and stirr'd by his conversation. I hear that you contemplate writing or speaking about him, and I wonder'd whether you had a picture of him. As I am the owner of two, I send you one."

Grand native growth

In a few days I go to lake Huron, and may have something to say of that region and people. From what I already see, I should say the young native population of Canada was growing up, forming a hardy, democratic, intelligent, radically sound, and just as American, good-natured and individualistic race, as the average range of best specimens among us. As among us, too, I please myself by considering that this element, though it may not be the majority, promises to be the leaven which must eventually leaven the whole lump.

A Zollverein between the U.S. and Canada

Some of the more liberal of the presses here are discussing the
question of a zollverein between the United States and Canada.
It is proposed to form a union for commercial purposes — to
altogether abolish the frontier tariff line, with its double sets of
custom house officials now existing between the two countries,
and to agree upon one tariff for both, the proceeds of this tariff
to be divided between the two governments on the basis of
population. It is said that a large proportion of the merchants of
Canada are in favor of this step, as they believe it would
materially add to the business of the country, by removing the
restrictions that now exist on trade between Canada and the
States. Those persons who are opposed to the measure believe
that it would increase the material welfare or the country, but it
would loosen the bonds between Canada and England; and this
sentiment overrides the desire for commercial prosperity.
Whether the sentiment can continue to bear the strain put upon
it is a question. It is thought by many that commercial
considerations must in the end prevail. It seems also to be
generally agreed that such a zollverein, or common customs
union, would bring practically more benefits to the Canadian
provinces than to the United States. (It seems to me a certainty
of time, sooner or later, that Canada shall form two or three
grand States, equal and independent, with the rest of the
American Union. The St. Lawrence and lakes are not for a
frontier line, but a grand interior or mid-channel.)

**Friday, June 18th, 1880**
**London, Ontario**

Calm and glorious roll the hours here the whole twenty-four. A
perfect day (the third in succession); the sun clear; a faint,
fresh, just palpable air setting in from the southwest;
temperature pretty warm at mid-day, but moderate enough
mornings and evenings. Everything growing well, especially
the perennials. Never have I seen verdure grass and trees and

bushery to greater advantage. All the accompaniments joyous.
Cat-birds, thrushes, robins, etc., singing. The profuse blossoms
of the tiger-lily (is it the tiger-lily?) mottling the lawns and
gardens everywhere with their glowing orange-red. Roses
everywhere, too.

A stately show of stars last night: the Scorpion erecting his
head of five stars, with glittering Antares in the neck, soon
stretched his whole length in the south; Arcturus hung
overhead; Vega a little to the east; Aquila lower down; the
constellation of the Sickle well toward setting; and the half-
moon, pensive and silvery, in the southwest.

### Saturday, June 19th, 1880
### London and Sarnia[xiii], Ontario

On the train from London to Sarnia 60 miles. A fine country,
many good farms, plenty of open land, the finest strips of
woods clean of underbrush some beautiful clusters of great
trees; plenty of fields with the stumps standing; some bustling
towns.

Sunset on the St. Clair. I am writing this on Front Street, close
by the river, the St. Clair, on a bank. The setting sun, a great
blood-red ball, is just descending on the Michigan shore,
throwing a bright crimson track across the water to where I
stand. The river is full of row-boats and shells, with their crews
of young fellows, or single ones, out practicing, a handsome,
inspiriting sight. Up north I see at Point Edward, on Canada
side, the tall elevator in shadow, with tall square turret, like
some old castle.

As I write, a long shell, with its crew of four stript to their
rowing shirts, sweeps swiftly past, the oars rattling in their
rowlocks.

Opposite, a little south, on the Michigan shore, stretches Port
Huron. It is a still, moist, voluptuous evening, the twilight
deepening apace. In the vapors fly bats and myriads of big

insects. A solitary robin is whistling his call, followed by mellow clucks, in some trees near. The panting of the locomotive and measured roll of cars comes from over shore, and occasionally an abrupt snort or screech, diffused in space. With all these utilitarian episodes, it is a lovely, soft, voluptuous scene, a wondrous half-hour for sunset, and then the long rose-tinged half-light with a touch of gray we sometimes have stretched out in June at day-close. How musical the cries and voices floating in from the river. Mostly while I have been here I have noticed those handsome shells and oar-boats, some of them rowing superbly.

At nearly nine it is still quite light, tempered with blue film, but the boats, the river, and the Michigan shores quite palpable. The rose color still falls upon everything. A big river steamer is crawling athwart the stream, hoarsely hissing. The moon in its third quarter is just up behind me. From over in Port Huron come the just-heard sounds of a brass band, practicing. Many objects half-burnt hulls, partially sunk wrecks, slanting or upright poles throw their black shadows in strong relief on the clear glistering water.

**Sunday, June 20ᵗʰ, 1880**
**Sarnia, Ontario**

A far-off reminiscence

I see today in a New York paper an account of the tearing down of old St. Ann's Church, Sands and Washington streets, Brooklyn, to make room for the East River Bridge landing and roadway. Away off, nearly 1000 miles distant, it roused the queerest reminiscences, which I feel to put down here.

*St Ann's Church, Brooklyn*

St. Ann's was twined with many memories of youth to me. I
think the church was built about 1824, the time when I (a little
child of six years) was first taken to live in Brooklyn, and I
remember it so well then and for long years afterwards. It was a
stately building with its broad grounds and grass, and the
aristocratic congregation, and the good clergyman, Mr.
Mcllvaine[xiv] (afterwards bishop of Ohio), and the long edifice
for Sunday-school (I had a pupil's desk there), and the fine
gardens and many big willow and elm trees in the
neighborhood. From St. Ann's started, over 50 years ago, a
strange and solemn military funeral, of the officers and sailors
killed by the explosion of the steamer Fulton at the Brooklyn
Navy Yard. I remember well the impressive services and the
dead march of the band (moving me even then to tears), and the
led horses and officer's trappings in the procession, and the
black-draped flags, and the old sailors, and the salutes over the
grave in the ancient cemetery in Fulton Street just below Tillary[xv]
(now all built over by solid blocks of houses and busy stores). I

was at school at the time of the explosion and heard the rumble which jarred half the city.

Nor was St. Ann's (Episcopal) the only church bequeathing Old Brooklyn reminiscences. Just opposite, within a stone's throw, on Sands Street, with a high range of steps, stood the main Methodist church, always drawing full congregations (always active, singing and praying in earnest), and the scene of the powerful revivals of those days (often continued for a week night and day without intermission). This latter was the favorite scene of the labors of John N. Maffitt[xvi], the famous preacher of his denomination. It was a famous church for pretty girls.

The history of those two churches would be a history of Brooklyn and of a main part of its families for the earlier half of the nineteenth century.

## Monday, June 21st, 1880
## Sarnia, Ontario

A moonlight excursion up Lake Huron

We were to start at 8 P.M., but after waiting forty minutes later for a music band, which to my secret satisfaction didn't come, we, and the Hiawatha went off without it.

Point Edward on the Canada side and Fort Gratiot on the Michigan, the crossing-line for the Grand Trunk RR, and looking well-alive with lights and the sight of shadowy moving cars were quickly passed between by our steamer, after pressing through currents of rapids for a mile along here, very dashy and inspiriting, and we were soon out on the wide sea room of the Lake. The far and faint-dim shores, the cool night-breeze, the plashing of the waters, and most of all the well-up moon, full and round and refulgent, were the features of this pleasant water-ride, which lasted till midnight.

During the day I had seen the magnificent steamboat, City of Cleveland[xvii], come from above, and, after making a short stop at Port Huron opposite, sped on her swift and stately way down the St. Clair.

*The City of Cleveland*

She plies between Cleveland and Duluth, and was on her return from the latter place; makes the voyage in three (?) days. At a Sarnia wharf I saw the Asia, a large steamboat for Lake Superior trade and passengers; understood there were three other boats on the line. Between Sarnia and Port Huron some nice small-sized ferry-boats are constantly plying. I went aboard the 'Dormer' and made an agreeable hour's jaunt to and fro.

A Sarnia Public School

Stopt impromptu at the school in George (?) where I saw crowds of boys out at recess, and went in without ceremony among them, and so inside for twenty minutes to the school, at its studies, music, grammar, etc. Never saw a healthier, handsomer, more intelligent or decorous collection of boys and girls, some 500 altogether. This twenty minute's sight, and what it inferred, are among my best impressions and recollections of Sarnia.

Went down to an Indian settlement at Ah-me-je-wah-noong (i.e., the Rapids) to visit the Indians, the Chippewas. Not much to see of novelty in fact nothing at all of aboriginal life or personality; but I had a fine drive with the gentleman that took me Dr. McLane[xviii], the physician appointed by the government for the tribe. There is a long stretch, three or four miles, fronting the St. Clair, south of Sarnia, running back easterly nearly the same distance, good lands for farming and rare sites for building and this is the 'reservation' set apart for these Chips. There are said to be four hundred of them, but I could not see evidences of one quarter of that number. There are three or four neat third-class wooden dwellings, a church, and council-house, but the less said about the rest of the edifices the better. "Every prospect pleases", as far as land, shore, and water are concerned, however. The Dominion government keeps entire faith with these people (and all its Indians, I hear), preserves these reservations for them to live on, pays them regular annuities, and, whenever any of their land is sold, puts the proceeds strictly in their funds. Here they farm languidly (I saw some good wheat), fish, etc.; but the young men generally go off to hire as laborers and deck-hands on the water. I saw and conversed with Wa-wa-nosh, the interpreter, son of a former chief. He talks and writes as well as I do. In a nice cottage nearby lived his mother, who doesn't speak anything but Chippewa. There are no very old people. I saw one man of thirty in the last stages of consumption. This beautiful and ample tract, in its present undeveloped condition, is quite an eyesore to the Sarnians.

**Thursday, June 24th, 1880**
**London, Ontario**

Tennyson's[xix] 'De Profundis'

Today I spent half an hour (in a recluse summer-house embowered) leisurely reading Tennyson's new poem 'De

Profundis.' I should call the piece (to coin a term) a specimen of the mystical-recherche and a mighty choice specimen. It has several exquisite little verses, not simple like rosebuds, but gem-lines like garnets or sapphires, cut by a lapidary artist. These for instance (someone has had a baby):

"O young life Breaking with laughter from the dark!"
"O dear Spirit half-lost In thine own shadow and this fleshly sign. That thou art thou who wailest being born."

Then from 'the Human Cry' attached:

"We feel we are nothing for all is Thou and in Thee;
We feel we are something that also has come from Thee."

Some cute friends afterward said it was altogether vague and could not be grasped. Very likely; it sounded to me like organ-playing, capriccio, which also cannot be grasped."

### Saturday, July 3rd, 1880
### London, Ontario

*Although Whitman does not mention it in his diary, we know that by this date he is not well. On July 1st, Dr Bucke writes to a friend that Whitman has not been well for a few days. Departure for the planned for 3 week excursion up into Quebec is delayed while Whitman recuperates.*

Night. Good night for stars and heavens; perfectly still and cloudless, fresh and cool enough; evenings very long; pleasant twilight till nine o'clock all through the last half of June and first half of July. These are my most pleasant hours. The air is pretty cool, but I find it enjoyable, and like to saunter the well-kept roads. Went out about 10 on a solitary ramble in the grounds, slow through the fresh air, over the gravel walks and velvety grass, with many pauses, many upward gazings. It was again an exceptional night for the show and sentiment of the stars, very still and clear, not a cloud, and neither warm nor cold. High overhead the constellation of the Harp; south of east

13

the Northern Cross; in the Milky Way the Diadem; and more to the north Cassiopeia; bright Arcturus and silvery Vega dominating aloft. But the heavens everywhere studded so thickly layers on layers of phosphorescence, spangled with those still orbs, emulous, nestling so close, with such light and glow everywhere, flooding the soul.

### Sunday, July 4th, 1880
### London, Ontario

Sunday evening. A very enjoyable hour or two this evening. They sent for me to come down in the parlor to hear my friend M.E.L.[xx], a deaf and dumb young woman, give some recitations (of course by pantomime, not a word spoken). She gave first an Indian legend, the warriors, the women, the woods, the action of an old chief, etc., very expressive. But best of all, and indeed a wonderful performance, she rendered Christ stilling the tempest (from Luke, is it?)

### Tuesday, July 6th, 1880
### London, Ontario

Forenoon

— A beautiful calm summer forenoon as we sit here (MEL and myself) on the verandah of Dr Bucke's house — the pleasant view, the wheat & hay fields, the birds singing, the sun shining, in the pleasant breeze, and all.

Nature so perfect.

### Wednesday, July 7th, 1880
### London, Ontario

Haymaking

I go out every day two or three hours for the spectacle. A sweet, poetic, practical, busy sight. Never before such fine growths of clover and timothy everywhere as the present year; and I never

saw such large fields of rich grass as on this farm. I ride around
in a low easy basket-wagon drawn by a sagacious pony. We go
at random over the flat just mown layers and all around through
lanes and across fields. The smell of the cut herbage, the whirr
of the mower, the trailing swish of the horse-rakes, the forks of
the busy pitchers, and the loaders on the wagons I linger long
and long to absorb them all. Soothing, sane, odorous hours!
Two weeks of such.

It is a great place for birds. No gunning here, and no dogs or
cats allowed. I never before saw so many robins, nor such big
fellows, nor so tame. You look out over the lawn any time and
can see from four or five to a score of them hopping about. I
never before heard singing wrens (the common house wren, I
believe), either, to such advantage two of them, these times, on
the verandahs of different houses where I have been staying.
Such vigorous, musical, well-fibred little notes! (What must the
winter wren be, then? they say it is far ahead of this.)

### Thursday, July 8th, 1880
### London, Ontario

Haymaking

I am in the midst of haymaking, and, though but a looker-on, I
enjoy it greatly, untiringly, day after day. Any hour I hear the
sound of scythes sharpening, or the distant rattle of horse-
mowers, or see loaded wagons, high-piled, slowly wending
toward the barns; or, toward sundown, groups of tan-faced men
going from work. Today we are indeed at the height of it here
in Ontario.

### Saturday 10th, Sunday 11th, Monday 12th July 1880
### London, Ontario

The delphinium flower paramount and profuse with its clear
blue yellow lilies profusion of white verbenas, delicately
spotting the green lawns many straw-colored hollyhocks many
like roses — others pure white lots of them, beautiful, clusters

every-where on the thick dense hedge-lines aromatic cedars at
evening red Canadian ? honeysuckle roses have been in great
profusion but now flower

the fences, verandahs, gables covered with grape-vines and
ivies, honeysuckle — a certain clematis (the Jack Manni)
bursting all over with deep purple blossoms, each with its four
(or five) great leaves, tough — but delicate as some court
lady's dress, but tough and durable, day after day.... — I
afterwards saw a large six-leaved ? one of pure satin-like white
— as beautiful a flower as I ever beheld.

### Tuesday 13th and Wednesday 14th July 1880
### London, Ontario

The Virginia creeper

Canadian honeysuckle

petunia the little trumpet-shaped petunia with its red and white
quarterings

at night the aromatic smell of the white cedar

oceans of milk white verbenas, and countu (?)
oceans of salmon-colored and scarlet ones

vast spread of pure sky overhead, of lumped pearly hue, and
other vast spread, here in these spacious grounds, of well-kept,
close-cropt grassy lawns

### Sunday, July 18th, 1880
### London, Ontario

Swallow-Gambols

I spent a long time to-day watching the swallows an hour this
forenoon and another hour afternoon. There is a pleasant,
secluded, close-cropt grassy lawn of a couple of acres or over,

flat as a floor and surrounded by a flowery and bushy hedge, just off the road adjoining the house, a favorite spot of mine. Over this open grassy area immense numbers of swallows have been sailing, darting, circling, and cutting large or small 8's and S's, close to the ground, for hours today. It is evidently for fun altogether. I never saw anything prettier this free swallow-dance. They kept it up, too, the greater part of the day.

## Monday, July 26th, 1880
## London and Toronto, Ontario

*By this date Whitman's health has greatly improved, to the point that he and Dr. Bucke are able to start their travels in Canada with confidence. Two days prior, Whitman had written to his friend Peter Doyle, "Am all right again for me — was sick ab't three weeks — at times pretty bad — was taken well care of here…"*

Started this morning at 8.40 from London for Toronto, 120 miles by R.R. I am writing this on the cars, very comfortable. We are now (10-11 A. M.) passing through a beautiful country. Rained hard last night, and showery this morning; everything looking bright and green. I am enjoying the ride (in a big easy R.R. chair in a roomy car). The atmosphere cool, moist, just right, and the sky veiled. All pleasant fertile country, sufficiently diversified, frequent signs of land not long cleared, black stumps (often the fields fenced with the roots of them), patches of beautiful woods, beech, fine elms, thrifty apple orchards, the hay and wheat mostly harvested, barley begun, oats almost ready; some good farms (a little hilly between Dundas and Hamilton, and the same on to Toronto). Corn looking well, potatoes ditto; but the great show-charm of my ride is from the unfailing grass and woods.

Hamilton a bustling city.

As we approach Toronto everything looks doubly beautiful, especially the glimpses of blue Ontario's waters, sunlit, yet with a slight haze, through which occasionally a distant sail.

In Toronto at half-past one. I rode up on top of the omnibus with the driver. The city made the impression on me of a lively dashing place. The lake gives it its character.

### Tuesday, July 27th, 1880
### Toronto and Lake Ontario, Ontario

Front St, wholesale pretty solid and
Church street
King street, stores, ladies Shopping ('the Broadway')
Sherbourne st. Jarvis st &c long and elegant streets of semi-rural residences, many of them very costly and beautiful

The horse-chestnut is the prevalent tree: you see it everywhere.
The mountain ash now with its bunches of red berries.
Queen's Park
The Insane Asylum
Mercer's Reformatory for Females

Toronto University, with its Norman architecture, and ample grounds
Knox college
Mr Dent
Mr Tully the architect[xxi]

*An autograph signed in another hand:*

James W. Clocum
24 Macomb Avenue
Detroit
Michigan
Wagner Car Conductor

I write this in Toronto, aboard the steamboat the Algerian, two o'clock P.M.

*The Algerian*

We are presently off.

The boat from Lewiston, New York, has just come in; the usual hurry with passengers and freight, and, as I write, I hear the pilot's bells, the thud of hawsers unloosened, and feel the boat squirming slowly from her ties, out into freedom. We are off, off into Toronto Bay (soon the wide expanse and cool breezes of Lake Ontario). As we steam out a mile or so we get a pretty view of Toronto from the blue foreground of the waters, — the whole rising spread of the city, groupings of roofs, spires, trees, hills in the background. Goodbye, Toronto, with your memories of a very lively and agreeable visit.

## A day and night on Lake Ontario

*Whitman and Bucke are travelling by boat from Toronto to Kingston at this point in their travels.*

We start from Toronto about 2 p m. in the Hamilton and Quebec steamboat — middling good-sized and comfortable, carrying shore freight and summer passengers. Quite a voyage — the whole length of Lake Ontario — very enjoyable day — clear, breezy, and cool enough for me to wrap my blanket around me as I pace the upper deck. For the first sixty or seventy miles we keep near the Canadian shore — of course no

19

land in sight the other side; stop at Port Hope, Coburg, etc., and
then stretch out toward the mid-waters of the lake.

I pace the deck or sit till pretty late, wrapt in my blanket,
enjoying all, — the coolness, darkness, — and then to my berth
awhile.

### Wednesday, July 28th, 1880
### Lake Ontario and Kingston, Ontario

Rose soon after three to come out on deck and enjoy a
magnificent night-show before dawn. Overhead the moon at
her half, and waning half, with lustrous Jupiter and Saturn,
made a trio-cluster close together in the purest of skies — with
the groups of the Pleiades and Hyades following a little to the
east. The lights off on the islands and rocks, the splashing
waters, the many shadowy shores and passages through them in
the crystal atmosphere, the dawn-streaks of faint red and yellow
in the east, made a good hour for me. We landed on Kingston
wharf just at sunrise.

Lake Ontario

Lake O. is 234 feet above sea-level (Huron is over 500, and
Superior over 600). The chain of lakes and river St. Lawrence
drain 400,000 square miles. The rainfall on this vast area
averages annually a depth of thirty inches — so that the
existence and supply of the river, fed by such inland preceding
seas, is a matter of very simple calculation after all."

Today Dr. M [etcalf]ˣˣⁱⁱtook me in his steam-yacht a long,
lively, varied voyage down among the Lakes of the Thousand
Islands. We went swiftly on east of Kingston, through cuts,
channels, lagoons (?) and out across lakes; numbers of islands
always in sight; often, as we steamed by, some almost grazing
us; rocks and cedars; occasionally a camping party on the
shores, perhaps fishing; a little sea-swell on the water; on our
return evening deepened, bringing a miracle of sunset.

I could have gone on thus for days over the savage-tame beautiful element. We had some good music (one of Verdi's compositions) from the band of B battery as we hauled in shore, anchored, and listened in the twilight (to the slapping rocking gurgle of our boat). Late when we reached home.

## Thursday, July 29th, 1880
## Kingston, Ontario

This forenoon a long ride through the streets of Kingston and so out into the country and the lake-shore road. Kingston is a military station (B battery), shows quite a fort, and half a dozen old martello towers (like big conical-topt pound cakes). It is a pretty town of fifteen thousand inhabitants.

## Saturday, July 31st, 1880
## Lakes of the Thousand Islands, New York

Evening, Saturday, Lakes of the Thousand Islands. I am writing this at and after sundown in the central portion ('American side,' as they call it here) of the Lakes of the Thousand Islands, twenty-five miles east of Kingston. The scene is made up of the most beautiful and ample waters, twenty or thirty woody and rocky islands (varying in size, some large, others small, others middling), the distant shores of the New York side, some puffing steamboats in the open waters, and numerous skiffs and row-boats, all showing as minute specks in the amplitude and primal naturalness.

The brooding waters, the cool and delicious air, the long evening with its transparent half-lights, the glistening and faintly slapping waves, the circles of swallows gambolling and piping.

## Sunday, August 1st, 1880
## Lakes of the Thousand Islands, Ontario

Sunday noon. Still among the Thousand Islands. This is about the centre of them, stretching twenty-five miles to the east and the same distance west. The beauty of the spot all through the day, the sunlit waters, the fanning breeze, the rocky and cedar-bronzed islets, the larger islands with fields and farms, the white-winged yachts and shooting row-boats, and over all the blue sky arching copious — make a sane, calm, eternal picture, to eyes, senses, and my soul.

Evening. An unusual show of boats gaily darting over the waters in every direction; not a poor model among them, and many of exquisite beauty and grace and speed. It is a precious experience, one of these long midsummer twilights in these waters arid this atmosphere. Land of pure air! Land of unnumbered lakes! Land of the islets and the woods!"

## Monday, August 2nd, 1880
## Lakes of the Thousand Islands and Kingston, Ontario
Early morning; a steady southwest wind; the fresh peculiar atmosphere of the hour and place worth coming a thousand miles to get. O'er the waters the gray rocks and dark-green cedars of a score of big and little islands around me; the added splendor of sunrise. As I sit, the sound of slapping water, to me most musical of sounds.

One peculiarity as you go about among the islands, or stop at them, is the entire absence of horses and wagons. Plenty of small boats, however, and always very handsome ones. Even the women row and sail skiffs. Often the men here build their boats themselves.

Forenoon. A run of three hours (some thirty miles) through the islands and lakes in the Princess Louise to Kingston.

*The Princess Louise*

Saw the whole scene, with its sylvan rocky and aquatic loveliness, to fine advantage. Such amplitude room enough here for the summer recreation of all North America.

**Tuesday, August 3ʳᵈ, 1880**

Left Kingston 6 A. M; arrived at Montreal same evening.

**Wednesday, August 4ᵗʰ, 1880**
**Montreal, Quebec**

In Montreal; guest of Dr. T. S. H[xxiii].

*Dr. Thomas Sterry Hunt*

Genial host, delightful quarters, good sleep. Explore the city
leisurely, but quite thoroughly: St. James Street, with its
handsome shops; Victoria Bridge; great French church; the
English Cathedral; the old French church of Notre Dame de
Bon Secours; the handsome, new, peculiarly and lavishly
ornamented church of Notre Dame de Lourdes; the French
streets of middle life, with their signs. A city of 150,000
people.

But the principal character of Montreal, to me, was from a drive
along the street looking down on the river front and the
wharves, where the steamships lay, — twenty or more of them,
— some as handsome and large as I ever saw; beautiful models,
trim, two or three hundred feet long; some moving out, one or
two coming in; plenty of room, and fine dockage, with heavy
masonry banks.

**Thursday, August 5th, 1880**
**Montreal, Quebec**

Forenoon. Three hours on Mount Royal, the great hill and park back of Montreal; spent the forenoon in a leisurely most pleasant drive on and about the hill; many views of the city below; the waters of the St. Lawrence in the clear air; the Adirondacks fifty miles or more distant; the excellent roads, miles of them, uphill and down; the plentiful woods, oak, pine, hickory; the French signboards <u>Passez a Droite</u> as we zigzag around; the splendid views, distances, waters, mountains, vistas, some of them quite unsurpassable; the continual surprises of fine trees, in groups or singly; the grand rocky natural escarpments; frequently open spaces, larger or smaller, with patches of goldenrod or white yarrow, or along the road the red fire-weed or Scotch thistle in bloom; just the great hill itself, with its rocks and trees unmolested by any impertinence of ornamentation.

Left Montreal; down to Quebec in steamer Montreal.

**Friday, August 6th, 1880**
**St Lawrence River and Saguenay River, Quebec**

Sunrise, the St. Lawrence near Quebec. Have just seen sunrise (standing on the extreme bow of the boat), the great round dazzling ball straight ahead over the broad waters, a rare view. The shores pleasantly, thickly, dotted with houses, the river here wide and looking beautiful in the golden morning's sheen. As we advance northeast the earth-banks high and sheer, quite thickly wooded; thin dawn-mists quickly resolving; the youthful, strong, warm forenoon over the high green bluffs; little white houses seen along the banks as we steam rapidly through the verdure; occasionally a pretensive mansion, a mill, a two-tower'd church (in burnish'd tin). A pretty shore (miles of it, sitting up high, well-sprinkled with dwellings of habitans, — farmers, fishermen, French cottagers, etc.), verdant everywhere (but no big trees) for fifty miles before coming to Quebec. These little rural cluster-towns just back from the bank-bluffs, so happy and peaceful looking. I saw them through my glass, everything quite minutely and fully. In one such town of perhaps two hundred houses on sloping ground, the old church with glistening spire stood in the middle, and quite a large graveyard around it. I could see the white head stones almost plainly enough to count them.

Approaching Quebec, rocks and rocky banks again, the shores lined for many miles with immense rafts and logs and partially hewn timber, the hills more broken and abrupt, the higher shores crowded with many fine dormer-window'd houses. Sail-ships appear in clusters with their weather-beaten spars and furl'd canvas. The river still ample and grand, the banks bold, plenty of round turns and promontories, plenty of gray rock cropping out. Rafts, rafts, of logs everywhere. The high rocky citadel thrusts itself out — altogether perhaps (at any rate as you approach it on the water, the sun two hours high) as picturesque an appearing city as there is on earth.

*Quebec City, 1880*

To the east of Quebec we pass the large fertile island of Orleans — the fields divided in long lateral strips across the island and appearing to be closely cultivated. In one field I notice them getting in the hay, a woman assisting, loading and hauling it. The view and scene continue broad and beautiful under the forenoon sun; around me an expanse of waters stretches fore and aft as far as I can see; outlines of mountains in the distance north and south; of the farthest ones the bulk and the crest lines showing through strong but delicate haze like gray lace.

Night we are steaming up the Saguenay.

### Saturday, August 7th, 1880
### Saguenay River, Quebec

Cold — overcoat — had a good night's sleep but up before sunrise — northern lights every night
As with overcoat on, or wrapt in my blanket I plant myself on the forward deck

have had my fill, the last three days of some of the tallest savagest scenery on earth.

I am here nearly 1000 miles slightly east of due north from Philadelphia, away up the Saguenay river in the strangest region you ever see. Am writing this on the steamer where I sleep and eat for a week — have just had a good breakfast, & am feeling well, for me — a beautiful sunny crispy day day — just right from the mountains and gray rocks in sight everywhere — the river, very fine flowing through all, but the water black ink — a dark brown sometimes like the boat has been — the crowd of people at Ha-ha bay here as we get ready to start all sorts ages, on the wharf, a good study to me — all speak French you know, (four fifths of this Quebec province French) where I am now travelling.

## The Savage Saguenay

Up these black waters, over a hundred miles — always strong, deep, (hundreds of feet, sometimes thousands,) ever with high, rocky hills for banks, green and gray — at times a little like some parts of the Hudson, but much more pronounc'd and defiant. The hills rise higher — keep their ranks more unbroken. The river is straighter and of more resolute flow, and its hue, though dark as ink, exquisitely polish'd and sheeny under the August sun. Different, indeed, this Saguenay from all other rivers — different effects — a bolder, more vehement play of lights and shades. Of a rare charm of singleness and simplicity. (Like the organ-chant at midnight from the old Spanish convent, in 'Favorita'[xxiv] — one strain only, simple and monotonous and unornamented — but indescribably penetrating and grand and masterful.) Great place for echoes: while our steamer was tied at the wharf at Tadousac (taj-oo-sac) waiting, the escape-pipe letting off steam, I was sure I heard a band at the hotel up in the rocks — could even make out some of the tunes. Only when our pipe stopp'd, I knew what caused it. Then at cape Eternity and Trinity rock, the pilot with his whistle producing similar marvellous results, echoes indescribably weird, as we lay off in the still bay under their shadows.

*Tadousac village, Quebec, Canada*

The priests

Saw them on every boat and at every landing; at Tadousac
came a barge and handsome yacht, manned and evidently
owned by them, to bring some departing passengers of their
cloth and take on others. It looked funny to me at first to see the
movements, ropes and tillers handled by these swarming black
birds, but I soon saw that they sailed their craft skillfully and
well.

Simple, middling industrious, merry, devout Catholic, a church
everywhere (priests in their black gowns everywhere, often
groups of handsome young fellows), life tones low, few
luxuries, none of the modern improvements, no hurry, often big
families of children, nobody 'progressive,' all apparently living
and moving entirely among themselves, taking small interest in
the outside world of politics, changes, news, fashions;
industrious, yet taking life very leisurely, with much dancing
and music.

## The inhabitants — good living

The inhabitants peculiar to our eyes; many marked characters, looks, by-plays, costumes, etc., that would make the fortune of actors who could reproduce them.

more or less aquatic character runs through the people. The two influences of French and British contribute a curious by play.

Grim and rocky and black-water'd as the demesne hereabout is, however, you must not think genial humanity, and comfort, and good-living are not to be met. Before I began this memorandum I made a first-rate breakfast of sea-trout, finishing off with wild raspberries. I find smiles and courtesy everywhere — physiognomies in general curiously like those in the United States — (I was astonish'd to find the same resemblance all through the province of Quebec.) In general the inhabitants of this rugged country (Charlevoix, Chicoutimi and Tadousac counties, and lake St. John region) a simple, hardy population, lumbering, trapping furs, boating, fishing, berry-picking and a little farming. I was watching a group of young boatmen eating their early dinner — nothing but an immense loaf of bread, had apparently been the size of a bushel measure, from which they cut chunks with a jack-knife. Must be a tremendous winter country this, when the solid frost and ice fully set in.

## Capes Eternity & Trinity

trinity rock
Cape Eternity

great calm eternal rock
everywhere a matted green
covering the mountain sides

But the great, haughty, silent capes themselves; I doubt if any crack points, or hills, or historic places of note, or anything of the kind elsewhere in the world, outvies these objects — (I

write while I am before them face to face.) They are very
simple, they do not startle — at least they did not me — but
they linger in one's memory forever. They are placed very near
each other, side by side, each a mountain rising flush out of the
Saguenay. A good thrower could throw a stone on each in
passing — at least it seems so. Then they are as distinct in form
as a perfect physical man or a perfect physical woman. Cape
Eternity is bare, rising, as just said, sheer out of the water,
rugged and grim (yet with an indescribable beauty) nearly two
thousand feet high. Trinity rock, even a little higher, also rising
flush, top-rounded like a great head with close-cut verdure of
hair. I consider myself well repaid for coming my thousand
miles to get the sight and memory of the unrivall'd duo. They
have stirr'd me more profoundly than anything of the kind I
have yet seen. If Europe or Asia had them, we should certainly
hear of them in all sorts of sent-back poems, rhapsodies, &c., a
dozen times a year through our papers and magazines.

*Capes Eternity and Trinity, Saguenay River, Quebec, Canada*

On the Saguenay

Contrasts all the while. At this place, backed by these
mountains high and bold, nestled down the hamlet of St. Pierre,

31

apparently below the level of the bay, and very secluded and cosy. Then two or three miles further on I saw a larger town high up on the plateau.

At St. Paul's Bay a stronger cast of scenery, many rugged peaks.

## The noticeable items on land

The long boxes of blueberries (we had over a thousand of them carried on board at Ha Ha Bay one day I was on the pier); the groups of 'boarders' (retaining all their most refined toggery); the vehicles, some 'calashes,' many queer old one-horse top-wagons with an air of faded gentility, the sail craft and steamers we pass — out in the stream; the rolling and turning up of the white-bellied porpoises; some special island or rock (often very picturesque in color or form) — all the scenes at the piers as we land to leave or take passengers and freight, especially many of the natives

the changing aspect of the light and the marvellous study from that alone every hour of the day or night; the indescribable sunsets and sunrises (I often see the latter now); the glorious nights and starts, Arcturus and Vega and Jupiter and Saturn, and the constellation of the scorpion — the scenes at breakfast and other meal-times (and what an appetite one gets!) — the delicious fish (I mean from the cook's fire, hot).

I had a good opera glass, and made constant use of it, sweeping every shore.

## Chicoutimi & Ha-Ha Bay

No indeed — life and travel and memory have offer'd and will preserve to me no deeper-cut incidents, panorama, or sights to cheer my soul, than these at Chicoutimi and Ha-ha bay, and my days and nights up and down this fascinating savage river — the rounded mountains, some bare and gray, some dull red, some draped close all over with matted green verdure or vines

— the ample, calm, eternal rocks everywhere — the long streaks of motley foam, a milk-white curd on the glistening breast of the stream — the little two-masted schooner, dingy yellow, with patch'd sails, set wing-and-wing, nearing us, coming saucily up the water with a couple of swarthy, black-hair'd men aboard — the strong shades falling on the light gray or yellow outlines of the hills all through the forenoon, as we steam within gunshot of them — while ever the pure and delicate sky spreads over all. And the splendid sunsets, and the sights of evening — the same old stars, (relatively a little different, I see, so far north) Arcturus and Lyra, and the Eagle, and great Jupiter like a silver globe, and the constellation of the Scorpion. Then northern lights nearly every night.

**Sunday, August 8th, 1880**
**St Lawrence River and Quebec City, Quebec**

Quebec from the River. Imagine a high rocky hill (the angles each a mile long), flush and bold to the river, with plateau on top, the front handsomely presented to the south and east (we are steaming up the river); on the principal height, still flush with the stream, a vast stone fort, the most conspicuous object in view; the magnificent St. Lawrence itself — many hills and ascents and tall edifices shown at their best — and steeples — the handsome town of Point Levi opposite — a long low sea-steamer just hauling out.

John Richardson
A Battery
Citadel
Quebec

Sunday forenoon. A leisurely varied drive around the city, stopping a dozen times and more. I went into the citadel, talked with the soldiers (over 100 here, Battery A, Canadian militia, the regulars having long since departed; a fort under the old dispensation, strong and picturesque as Gibraltar). Then to several Catholic churches and to the Esplanade.

The chime-bells rang out at intervals all the forenoon, joyfully clanging. It seems almost an art here. I never before heard their peculiar sound to such mellifluous advantage and pleasure. The old name of Quebec — Hochelega.[xxv]

## Monday, August 9th, 1880
## Quebec City, Montmorenci Falls and Montreal, Quebec

Forenoon. We have driven out six or seven miles to the Montmorenci Falls, and I am writing this as I sit high up on the steps, the cascade immediately before me, the great rocky chasm at my right and an immense lumber depot bordering the river, far, far below, almost under me, to the left. It makes a pretty and picturesque show, but not a grand one. The principal fall, 30 or 40 feet wide and 250 high, pours roaring and white down a slant of dark gray rocks, and there are six or seven rivulet falls flanking it.

Since writing the above I have gone down the steps (some 350) to the foot of the Fall, which I recommend every visitor to do: the view is peculiar and fine. The whole scene grows steadily upon one, and I can imagine myself, after many visits, forming a finally first-class estimate, from what I see here of Montmorenci over a part of the scaly, grim, bald-black rock, the water falling downward like strings of snowy-spiritual beautiful tresses.

*Montmorenci Falls, Quebec, Canada*

The road out here from the city is a very good one, lined with moderate-class houses, copious with women and children. Doors and windows wide open, exhibiting many groups to us as we passed. The men appear to be away: I wonder what they work at? Every house for miles is set diagonally with one of its corners to the road, never its gable or front. There seems little farming here, and I see no factories.

Through the forenoon watched the cascade under the advantages now of partly cloudy atmosphere and now of the full sunshine.
The tamarack-trees.
the great loaves of bread,
shaped like clumsy
butterflies.

———

Jo Le Clerc
— our driver
lifting his fingers

———

groups
onions

houses all set diagonally
long strips
good kitchen cordins (?)

hundreds of (to our eyes) funny-looking one-horse vehicles, —
calashes; antique gigs.

Long narrow strips of farms (?) — heavy two-seated covered
voitures, always drawn by one horse.

coarse rank tobacco

—

big-roofed one-story houses with projecting eaves

—

potatoes, plenty and fine-looking.

—

entire absence of barns

doors & windows wide open, exhibiting (?) many groups to us
as we passed

—

the ruins of Montcalm's[xxvi] country-seat, the strong old stone
walls still standing to the second story; indeed, many old stone
walls, including those of the old city, still standing.

Very pleasant journey of 180 miles this afternoon and tonight;
crowds of Catholic priests onboard with their long loose black
gowns, and the broad brims of their hats turned into a peculiar
triangle.

### Tuesday, August 10th, 1880
### Montreal and St Lawrence River, Quebec

Again in Montreal. As I write this I am seated aft in the
delicious river breeze on the steamboat[xxvii] that is to take me
back west some ? 380 miles from here to Hamilton. Two hours
yet before we start; few passengers, as they come east by the
boats, and then generally take the railroad back. Montreal has

the largest show of sail ships and handsome ocean steamers of any place on the river and lake line, and I am right in full sight of them.

Going on the river westward from Montreal is pretty slow and tedious, taking a long time to get through the canals and many locks, to Lake St. Francis, where the steamer emerges to the river again. These rapids along here — the boats can descend, but cannot go up them. A great inconvenience to the navigator, but they are quite exciting with their whirls and roar and foam, and very picturesque.

—

(Always accenting the last syllable with a tremendous <u>bah</u>!)

— here, too, are graveyards. In a lovely little shore-nook, under an apple-tree, green, grassy, fenced by rails, lapped by the waters, I saw a grave, white headstone and foot-stone; could almost read the inscription.

Evening. Wondrously clear, pleasant, and calm. I think it must have been unusual; the river was as smooth as glass for hours. All the stars shone in it from below as brightly as above, — the young moon, and Arcturus, and Aquila, and, after 10, lustrous Jupiter. Nothing could be more exquisite. I sat away forward by the bow & watched the show till after 11.

## Thursday, August 12th, 1880
## Toronto and Hamilton, Ontario

Arrived in Toronto; 3 hours at Queen's Hotel; left 11 A. M.

*Queen's Hotel, Toronto, Canada*

As we take the cars at Toronto to go west, the first thing I notice is the change of temperature; no more the cool fresh air of the lakes, the St. Lawrence, and the Saguenay.

4-1/2 P.M. I am writing this at Hamilton, high up on a hill south of the town.

**Friday, August 13th, 1880**
**Hamilton, Ontario**

P. M. I write this on a singular strip of beach off Hamilton.

Today have been driving about for several hours, some of the roads high up on the crest of the mountain; spent a pleasant hour in the wine vaults of Mr. Haskins[xxviii], and another at the vineyard and hospitable house of Mr. Paine, who treated us to some delicious native wine.

**Monday, August 16th, 1880**
**Hamilton and London, Ontario**

I am writing this on the high balcony of the Asylum[xxix] at Hamilton (Ontario, Canada). The city is spread in full view before me. (Is there not an escaped patient? I see a great commotion, Dr. W. and several attendants, men and women, rushing down the cliff). A dark, moist, lowering forenoon; balmy air though; wind southwest.

5-1/2 P.M. Arrived back in London a couple of hours ago, all right. Am writing this in my room, Dr. B.'s house.

Along the way on the journey from Hamilton to London everywhere through the car-windows I saw locust-trees growing and the broad yellow faces of sunflowers, the sumach bushes with their red cones, and the orchard trees loaded with apples.

**Saturday, August 21st, 1880**
**London, Ontario**

I rose this morning at four and look'd out on the most pure and refulgent starry show. Right over my head, like a Tree-Universe spreading with its orb-apples, — Aldebaran leading the Hyades; Jupiter of amazing lustre, softness, and volume; and, not far behind, heavy Saturn, — both past the meridian; the seven sparkling gems of the Pleiades; the full moon, voluptuous and yellow, and full of radiance, an hour to setting in the west. Everything so fresh, so still; the delicious something there is in early youth, in early dawn — the spirit, the spring, the feel; the air and light, precursors of the untried sun; love, action, forenoon, noon, life — full-fibred, latent with them all. And is not that Orion the mighty hunter? Are not those the three glittering studs in his belt? And there to the north Capella and his kids.

**Sunday, August 29th, 1880**
**London, Ontario**

At Dr. B.'s. The robins on the grassy lawn (I sometimes see a dozen at a time, great fat fellows). The little black-and-yellow bird with his billowy flight [the goldfinch]; the flocks of sparrows —

# WHAT NEXT? WHITMAN'S LIFE AFTER THE DIARY ENDS

This is the last diary entry that Whitman writes during his time in Canada. We know that he leaves the Buckes' house at the end of September. It's not clear why he stays so long after the end of the trip. Perhaps he simply liked being there. He never went back and letters suggest that, always unknown to Whitman, Bucke's more conventional wife Jessie wasn't quite so keen on Whitman as her husband was. She had 8 children and Whitman had stayed with the Buckes for four months, excluding the three weeks that Whitman and Bucke were on their travels. At any rate, Bucke accompanies Whitman as far as Niagara Falls on the journey home and Whitman judges his summer a great success. He writes to his friend Edward Carpenter[xxx] on Tuesday, September 28th from Niagara Falls,

"I am now on my way back home to Camden, stopping here only a short time. I am feeling heartier physically than for years."

He is to live for another 11 years.

Once home, his life continues busily. He visits old friends and develops new friendships. He keeps in touch with many people through his steady letter-writing. Oscar Wilde visits him in January 1882 and they drink elderberry wine together.

In 1883 the Walt Whitman biography that Whitman co-authored with Bucke is published.

Whitman delivers a lecture about Lincoln several times. Notes[xxxi] contained along with his Canadian diary — as well as the diary itself — suggest that he had probably planned to deliver a lecture about Canada at some point. However, this did not happen.

He issues two new editions of Leaves of Grass. The first of these comes out in 1884 and sales from this enable him to leave his brother George's house and to buy his own at 328 Mickle Street, also in Camden. His departure causes a rift between the two brothers that is never fully made right.

*Whitman's house: 328 Mickle Street, Camden, New Jersey*

Mary Oakes Davis becomes Whitman's live-in housekeeper in 1885[xxxii].

*Mary Oakes Davis*

In 1888 Whitman has another paralytic stroke and is very ill. The stroke leaves him much more paralysed than before. He makes another will and names Bucke his chief literary executor. Whitman worries about the long-term care of his brother Eddie, who has learning difficulties. He leaves the vast majority of what he has to him.

In 1889, his housekeeper's foster son Warren 'Warry' Fritzinger[xxxiii] becomes Whitman's regular nurse and caretaker.

*Warry and Whitman on the dock at Camden in 1890*

In 1890, in response to a homoerotic analysis of his Calamus poems, Whitman claims to have fathered six illegitimate children. None of these children have ever been found or identified. In the same year, he commissions a grand $4k tomb for himself in Harleigh Cemetery, Camden.

He catches pneumonia in December of 1891, which leaves him further debilitated. In the afternoon of Saturday, March 26th, 1892 his health quite suddenly sinks still further. He dies at 645pm in the company of Warry, Mary and another nurse, Elizabeth Keller.[xxxiv]

On Wednesday, March 30th there is a public viewing of his body at Mickle Street from 11am to 2pm. More than one thousand people visit in three hours. Several thousand people line the street to watch the funeral procession. His funeral takes place at 3pm and his body is placed in its elaborate tomb.

There is a public ceremony during which there are music, speeches and refreshments. Whitman's friend Robert Ingersoll[xxxv], the famous lawyer, Civil War veteran and orator gives the eulogy[xxxvi].

*Whitman's tomb, Harleigh Cemetery, Camden,*
*on his funeral day*

# THE LIFE OF THE DIARY ITSELF

And what of the diary itself? What has its life been since Whitman created it?

Whitman did not customarily keep a diary and the diary that he kept during his summer in Canada does not look like a traditional diary.

There are two distinct parts to it.

The first part is written mainly on scraps of paper. It starts on June 4th, 1880 and goes to the end of July, the point at which Whitman and Bucke depart for their trip.

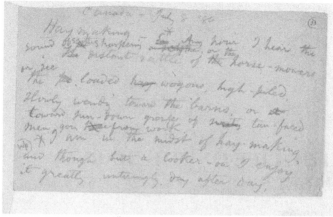

The second part is made out of larger bits of paper, stuck together by Whitman to form a notebook.

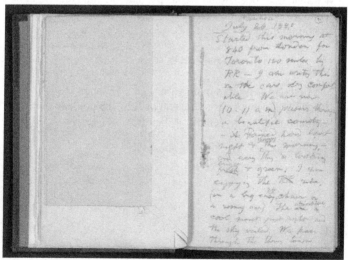

It is assumed that the diaries lived with Whitman until his death, at which point they went to Bucke, as Whitman's chief literary executor. Towards the end of 1900, a friend of Whitman and Bucke's named William Sloane Kennedy proposed to Bucke that they co-author a work about Whitman. Bucke was apparently keen but before they could get started, he slipped and hit his head on the icy floor of the veranda of his house at the London asylum and never regained consciousness. On Bucke's death, his son Edward sent the Canada diary to Kennedy who organised and transcribed the "worn and time-stained fragments of paper", publishing the first reading edition of the diary in 1904.

The original diaries made their way during the 20th Century to the prodigious Walt Whitman collector, Charles E. Feinberg. They are now held by the Library of Congress where they have been brilliantly digitised and are available to explore[xxxix].

In 1978, William White published a very precisely transcribed, academic version of the diary as part of a three part volume: The Collected Writings of Walt Whitman.

# THIS EDITION

It is strange that the last standalone, reading version of the diary was published in 1904 and then with a print run of only 500 copies. It is time to bring this little-known work to be brought into the light. Whitman has been dead since 1891 and that summer in Canada has passed well beyond the edges of living memory. The diary is a rare chance to time travel back to 1880, to hear Whitman's personal voice and to see as he saw.

**A note on the text**

All the words in this edition are Whitman's. The purpose has been to create something as readable and accessible as possible. In a few places there has been a slight reordering — to attach diary entries to dates and to give a clearer sense of the forward-moving narrative of the diary. Also included from this time are a few entries that appeared later in Specimen Days, Whitman's collection of notes, sketches and essays.

Whitman is not consistent with capitalisation in the diary. These inconsistencies have been left in as much as possible. He would sometimes register uncertainty about a choice of word by appending a question mark to it. These have also been left in.

# MAP, ENDNOTES AND PHOTOGRAPHS

## Map

This map shows Whitman's movements in that summer of 1880. You can visit an interactive version at: https://bit.ly/2MGEBMG

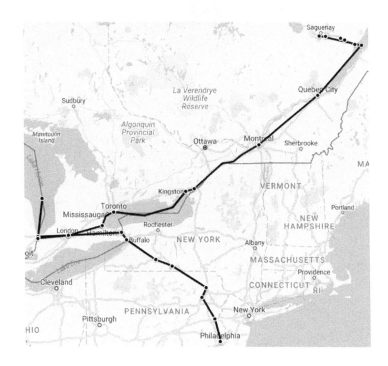

## Footnotes and Photographs

i Whitman's 1880 estate of $1800 is worth approximately $42000 in today's money.

ii Whitman's brother George Washington Whitman (1829 – 1901)

iii Sister-in-law Louisa Orr Whitman (1842 – 1892)

iv No photo survives of brother Edward Whitman (1835 – 1902).

v Dr. Richard Maurice Bucke (1837 – 1902), Whitman's close friend and host in Canada.

vi 9th and Green Streets Railroad Station, Philadelphia: the starting point of Whitman's journey into Canada.

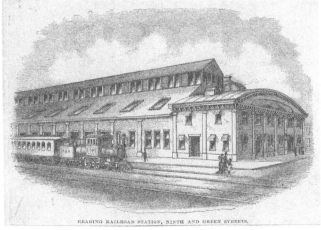

READING RAILROAD STATION, NINTH AND GREEN STREETS,

vii London Asylum for the Insane, Ontario, home of Dr Bucke, who was Chief Superintendent there.

viii Whitman joyfully remembers seeing a performance by Junius Brutus Booth (1796 – 1852), an English actor who emigrated to the United States in 1821. He starred in Richard III at the Bowery Theatre, New York. He was hugely famous and also troubled and an alcoholic. His son John Wilkes Booth assassinated Abraham Lincoln.

ix Whitman remembers hearing Marietta Alboni (1826 – 1894), Contralto opera singer. Starred in 'Norma' by Vincenzo Bellini in 1853.

x Dr Nelson Henry Beemer (1853 – 1934), First Physician at the London Asylum and someone that Whitman meets.

xi Elias Hicks (1748 – 1830) was a friend of Walt Whitman's father and grandfather. He was also a Quaker whose controversial preaching led to a split from the Religious Society of Friends in 1827.

xii Elisa Seaman Leggett (1815 – 1900). Suffragist and abolitionist, she wrote to Walt Whitman every so often, from 1880 until his death.

xiii In Sarnia Whitman stays with Timothy Blair Pardee QC,

Minister of Crown Lands.

xiv Whitman remembers hearing Charles Pettit McIlvaine (1799 – 1873) preach at St Ann's Church in Brooklyn. McIlvaine later became Bishop of Ohio.

xv The Whitmans lived on Tillary in Brooklyn; Walt Whitman's father Walter Whitman (a builder) built them a house there.

xvi Whitman also remembers in his childhood hearing the fiery Methodist preacher John Newland Maffitt (1795 – 1850), preaching at the Methodist church on Sands Street, Brooklyn.

xvii The City of Cleveland. Whitman saw admired this steamboat on Lake Huron.

xviii Whitman mentions a drive with a Dr. McLane during his time in Sarnia. There is no record of a Dr. McLane and it seems more likely to be a Dr McLean. The McLeans are a family still living in Sarnia today.

xix Lord Alfred Tennyson (1809 – 1892) The two poets wrote to each other and commented on each other's work.

xx Whitman mentions his friendship with a girl named 'M.E.L' at the asylum. We have not yet been able to discover who she was.

xxi In Toronto Whitman met Kivas Tully (1820 – 1905), an Irish-Canadian architect. Tully sent Whitman some maps after their meeting.

xxii Dr. William George Metcalf (1847 – 1885) was acting Superintendent of the Rockwood Asylum in Kingston at the time of the diary and Whitman stayed with him in Kingston. Metcalf was killed by a patient in 1885; stabbed in the abdomen on one of his rounds.

xxiii In Montreal Whitman stays with Dr. Thomas Sterry Hunt (1826 – 1892), a prominent geologist and chemist. Invented the green ink used on American banknotes. It was he who first introduced Whitman's writings to Dr. Bucke.

xxiv Whitman likens the quiet power of the Saguenay River to an organ chant in Gaetano Donizetti's (1797 – 1848) opera 'La Favorita', set in 14th Century Spain. Lovers fight for the hand of Leonora, 'the favorite'.

xxv Whitman mentions the old name of Quebec — Hochelaga (ho-shel'-a-gah). This is derived from an aboriginal word meaning beaver-grounds.

xxvi In his exploration of the area around Quebec City, Whitman mentions Louis-Joseph de Montcalm (1712 – 1759). Montcalm was Commander of the French forces, defending New France against the British. He lost both his life and Quebec to the British at the Battle of the Plains of Abraham in 1759.

xxvii Whitman and Bucke travel from Toronto to Kingston in the steamboat, The Algerian.

xxviii William Haskins, one of the earliest commercial grape growers in the region.

xxix Dr. Bucke had been medical superintendent of this asylum in 1876.

xxx Edward Carpenter; socialist poet, gay activist, philosopher (1844-1929)

Edwd. Carpenter

xxxi <u>Whitman's notes on Canada, kept with his Canadian diaries</u>
The waters, the lakes, and the indescribable grandeur of the St. Lawrence are the beauty of Canada through this vast line of two thousand miles and over. In its peculiar advantages, sanities, and charms, I doubt whether the globe for democratic purposes has its equal.

? For lecture — for conclusion ?

A grand, sane, temperate land, the amplest and most beautiful and stream of water, — a river and necklace of vast lakes, pure, sweet, eligible, supplied by the chemistry of millions of square miles of gushing springs and melted snows. No stream this for side frontier — stream rather for the great central current, the glorious mid-artery, of the great Free Pluribus Unum of America, the solid Nationality of the present and the future, the home of an improved grand race of men and women; not of some select class only, but of larger, saner, better masses. I should say this vast area (from lat. and) was fitted to be their unsurpassed habitat. I know nothing finer. The European democratic tourist, philanthropist, geographer, or genuine inquirer, will make a fatal mistake who leaves these shores without understanding this. — I know nothing finer, either from the point of view of the sociologist, the traveller, or the artist, than a month's devotion to even the surface of Canada, over the line of the great Lakes and the St. Lawrence, the fertile, populous, and happy province of Ontario, the [province] of Quebec, with another month to the hardy maritime regions of New Brunswick, Nova Scotia, and Newfoundland.

I see, or imagine I see in the future, a race of two million farm-families, ten million people every farm running down to the water, 1 or at least in sight of it the best air and drink and sky and scenery of the globe, the sure foundation-nutriment of heroic men and women. The summers, the winters I have sometimes doubted whether there could be a great race without the hardy influence of winters in due proportion.

Total Dominion, 3,500,000 square miles. Quebec, Ontario, Nova

Scotia, New Brunswick, Prince Edward Island, British Columbia, Manitoba, Hudson Bay, and Northwest Territories. (Newfoundland not in Dominion.) Area equal to the whole of Europe. Population, 1880, four to five millions.

Principal timber: white and red pine. The woods are full of white oak, elm, beech, ash, maple (bird's-eye, curled, etc.), walnut, cedar, birch, tamarack, sugar orchards (maple).

The honey-bee everywhere; rural ponds and lakes (often abounding with the great white sweet-smelling water-lily); wild fruits and berries everywhere; in the vast flat grounds the prairie anemone.

The fisheries of Canada are almost unparalleled... Then the furs...

If the most significant trait of modern civilization is benevolence (as a leading statesman has said), it is doubtful whether this is anywhere illustrated to a fuller degree than in the province of Ontario. All the maimed, insane, idiotic, blind, deaf and dumb, needy, sick and old, minor criminals, fallen women, foundlings, have advanced and ample provision of house and care and oversight, at least fully equal to anything of the kind in any of the United States — probably indeed superior to them. In Ontario for its eighty-eight electoral ridings, each one returning a member of parliament, there are four Insane Asylums, an Idiot Asylum, one Institution for the Blind, one for the Deaf and Dumb, one for Foundlings, a Reformatory for Girls, one for Women, and no end of homes for the old and infirm, for waifs, and for the sick. Its school system, founded on the Massachusetts plan, is one of the best and most comprehensive in the world.

Some of the good people of Ontario have complained in my hearing of faults and fraudulencies, commissive or emissive, on the part of the government, but I guess said people have reason to bless their stars for the general fairness, economy, wisdom, and liberality of their officers and administration.

June and July, Canada. Such a procession of long-drawn-out, delicious half-lights nearly every evening, continuing on till 'most 9 o'clock all through the last two weeks of June and the first two of July! It was worth coming to Canada to get these long-stretch'd sunsets in their temper'd shade and lingering, lingering twilights, if nothing more.

xxxii Mary Oakes Davis (1838 – 1908) was Whitman's live-in friend and housekeeper during his final years.

xxxiii Frederick Warren Fritzinger (1866 – 1899) looked after Whitman from 1899. He had been a sailor and was Mary Oakes Davis' foster son.

xxxiv Elizabeth Keller (1839 – ?) nursed Whitman during his final days and was present when he died.

xxxv Robert Ingersoll (1833 – 1899) was a friend of Whitman's and a famous lawyer, Civil War veteran and orator.

xxxvi <u>Robert Ingersoll's eulogy for Walt Whitman.</u>
Again, we, in the mystery of Life, are brought face to face with
the mystery of Death. A great man, a great American, the most
eminent citizen of this Republic, lies dead before us, and we have
met to pay tribute to his greatness and his worth.

I know he needs no words of mine. His fame is secure. He laid
the foundations of it deep in the human heart and brain. He was,
above all I have known, the poet of humanity, of sympathy. He
was so great that he rose above the greatest that he met without
arrogance, and so great that he stooped to the lowest without
conscious condescension. He never claimed to be lower or greater
than any of the sons of men.

He came into our generation a free, untrammeled spirit, with
sympathy for all. His arm was beneath the form of the sick. He
sympathized with the imprisoned and despised, and even on the
brow of crime he was great enough to place the kiss of human
sympathy.

One of the greatest lines in our literature is his, and the line is
great enough to do honor to the greatest genius that has ever
lived. He said, speaking of an outcast: "Not until the sun excludes
you will I exclude you."

His charity was as wide as the sky, and wherever there was human
suffering, human misfortune, the sympathy of Whitman bent
above it as the firmament bends above the earth.

He was built on a broad and splendid plan—ample, without
appearing to have limitations—passing easily for a brother of
mountains and seas and constellations; caring nothing for the
little maps and charts with which timid pilots hug the shore, but
giving himself freely with the recklessness of genius to winds and
waves and tides; caring for nothing so long as the stars were
above him. He walked among men, among writers, among verbal
varnishers and veneerers, among literary milliners and tailors, with
the unconscious majesty of an antique god.

He was the poet of that divine democracy which gives equal rights to all the sons and daughters of men. He uttered the great American voice; uttered a song worthy of the great Republic. No man has ever said more for the rights of humanity, more in favor of real democracy, of real justice. He neither scorned nor cringed; was neither tyrant nor slave. He asked only to stand the equal of his fellows beneath the great flag of nature, the blue and stars. He was the poet of life. It was a joy simply to breathe. He loved the clouds; he enjoyed the breath of morning, the twilight, the wind, the winding streams. He loved to look at the sea when the waves burst into the whitecaps of joy. He loved the fields, the hills; he was acquainted with the trees, with birds, with all the beautiful objects of the earth. He not only saw these objects, but understood their meaning, and he used them that he might exhibit his heart to his fellow-men.

He was the poet of Love. He was not ashamed of that divine passion that has built every home; that divine passion that has painted every picture and given us every real work of art; that divine passion that has made the world worth living in and has given some value to human life.

He was the poet of the natural, and taught men not to be ashamed of that which is natural. He was not only the poet of democracy, not only the poet of the great Republic, but he was the poet of the human race. He was not confined to the limits of this country, but his sympathy went out over the seas to all the nations of the earth.

He stretched out his hands and felt himself the equal of all kings and of all princes, and the brother of all men, no matter how high, no matter how low.

He has uttered more supreme words than any writer of our century, possibly of almost any other. He was, above all things, a man, and above genius, above all the snow-capped peaks of intelligence, above all art, rises the true man.

He was the poet of Death. He accepted all life and all death, and he justified all. He had the courage to meet all, and was great enough and splendid enough to harmonize all and to accept all there is as a divine melody.

You know better than I what his life has been, but let me say one thing: Knowing as he did, what others can know and what they can not, he accepted and absorbed all theories, all creeds, all religions, and believed in none. His philosophy was a sky that embraced all clouds and accounted for all clouds. He had a philosophy and a religion of his own, broader, as he believed—and as I believe—than others. He accepted all, he understood all, and he was above all.

He was absolutely true to himself. He had frankness and courage, and he was as candid as light. He was willing that all the sons of men should be absolutely acquainted with his heart and brain. He had nothing to conceal. Frank, candid, pure, serene, noble, and yet for years he was maligned and slandered, simply because he had the candor of nature. He will be understood yet, and that for which he was condemned—his frankness, his candor—will add to the glory and greatness of his fame.

He wrote a liturgy for mankind; he wrote a great and splendid psalm of life, and he gave to us the gospel of humanity—the greatest gospel that can be preached.

He was not afraid to live; not afraid to die. For many years he and Death lived near neighbors. He was always willing and ready to meet and greet this king called Death, and for many months he sat in the deepening twilight waiting for the night; waiting for the light.

He never lost his hope. When the mists filled the valleys, he looked upon the mountain tops, and when the mountains in darkness disappeared, fixed his gaze upon the stars.

In his brain were the blessed memories of the day and in his heart were mingled the dawn and dusk of life.

He was not afraid; he was cheerful every moment. The laughing nymphs of day did not desert him. They remained that they might clasp the hands and greet with smiles the veiled and silent sisters of the night. And when they did come, Walt Whitman stretched his hand to them. On one side were the nymphs of day, and on the other the silent sisters of the night, and so, hand in hand, between smiles and tears, he reached his journey's end.

From the frontier of life, from the western wave-kissed shore, he sent us messages of content and hope, and these messages seem now like strains of music blown by the "Mystic Trumpeter" from Death's pale realm.

To-day we give back to Mother Nature, to her clasp and kiss, one of the bravest, sweetest souls that ever lived in human clay. Charitable as the air and generous as Nature, he was negligent of all except to do and say what he believed he should do and should say.

And I to-day thank him, not only for you but for myself, for all the brave words he has uttered. I thank him for all the great and splendid words he has said in favor of liberty, in favor of man and woman, in favor of motherhood, in favor of fathers, in favor of children, and I thank him for the brave words that he has said of death.

He has lived, he has died, and death is less terrible than it was before. Thousands and millions will walk down into the "dark valley of the shadow" holding Walt Whitman by the hand. Long after we are dead the brave words he has spoken will sound like trumpets to the dying.

And so I lay this little wreath upon this great man's tomb. I loved him living, and I love him still.

xxxvii and xxxviii The original diaries are kept by the Library of Congress in the Manuscript Division as part of the collection of Walt Whitman Papers in the Charles E. Feinberg Collection

xxxix The original diaries have been brilliantly digitised and can be viewed online as follows.

First diary, June to July 1880:
https://www.loc.gov/item/mss1863000009

Second diary, August to September 1880:
https://www.loc.gov/item/mss1863000010

Made in the USA
Middletown, DE
18 May 2020